*Brief Authority*

Rebecca E. Pitts
1905–83

# BRIEF AUTHORITY

## Fragments of One Woman's Testament

### Rebecca E. Pitts

VANTAGE PRESS
New York / Washington / Atlanta
Los Angeles / Chicago

*Lines from "The History of Truth," by W. H. Auden, from* W. H. Auden: Collected Poems, *edited by Edward Mendelson,* ©*1976, reprinted by permission of Random House, Inc. Lines from Muriel Rukeyser used by permission of International Creative Management, Inc., Copyright 1944, 1972 by Muriel Rukeyser.*

FIRST EDITION

All rights reserved, including the right of reproduction in whole or in part in any form.

Copyright © 1986 by Allegra Stewart

Published by Vantage Press, Inc.
516 West 34th Street, New York, New York 10001

Manufactured in the United States of America
ISBN: 0-533-06760-X

Library of Congress Catalog Card No.: 85-90262

In memory of Estella Coffin Pitts

> *But man, proud man,*
> *Dressed in a little brief authority,*
> *Most ignorant of what he's most assured,*
> *His glassy essence, like an angry ape,*
> *Plays such fantastic tricks before high heaven*
> *As makes the angels weep.*
> —*Measure for Measure*

> *There are twin gates of Sleep, one of which is said to be of horn, whereby an easy exit is given to visions of the truth; the other is brilliant with white ivory, but the depths send up deceiving dreams.*
> —*Aeneid* VI, 893–96

> *We must put our arms round the vexatious world, whose true name is creation; only then do our fingers reach the realm of lightning and of grace. . . . Face the hour which approaches . . . the biographical and historical hour, just as it is, in its whole world content and apparently senseless contradiction, without weakening the impact of otherness in it.*
> —Martin Buber

> *There is no other spirit but that which is nourished by the unity of life and by unity with the world.*
> —Martin Buber

> *Continuous creation is thought of not only as a series of successive acts of creation, but also as the eternal presence of the* one *creative act.*
> —C. G. Jung

# CONTENTS

*Foreword*, by Allegra Stewart . . . . . . . . . . . . . . . . . . xi

Theater . . . . . . . . . . . . . . . . . . . . . . . . . . . . . . . . . 1
Program Note . . . . . . . . . . . . . . . . . . . . . . . . . . . . 2
Meditation . . . . . . . . . . . . . . . . . . . . . . . . . . . . . . 3

## The Dance

Soliloquy . . . . . . . . . . . . . . . . . . . . . . . . . . . . . . . 7
Strangers . . . . . . . . . . . . . . . . . . . . . . . . . . . . . . . 8
On Calypso's Island . . . . . . . . . . . . . . . . . . . . . . . . 9
A Dream of Meaning . . . . . . . . . . . . . . . . . . . . . . 10
Sea Figure . . . . . . . . . . . . . . . . . . . . . . . . . . . . . 12
Song for a Voyager . . . . . . . . . . . . . . . . . . . . . . . 15
The Horn Gate . . . . . . . . . . . . . . . . . . . . . . . . . . 16
Prisoner . . . . . . . . . . . . . . . . . . . . . . . . . . . . . . 18
Cobra Goddess . . . . . . . . . . . . . . . . . . . . . . . . . . 19
Setting Out . . . . . . . . . . . . . . . . . . . . . . . . . . . . 20
Advent and Eleusis . . . . . . . . . . . . . . . . . . . . . . . 22
Star . . . . . . . . . . . . . . . . . . . . . . . . . . . . . . . . . 25

## The World in Our Heart

On the Beach . . . . . . . . . . . . . . . . . . . . . . . . . . 29
Hieroglyphics . . . . . . . . . . . . . . . . . . . . . . . . . . 30
Hunter Moon . . . . . . . . . . . . . . . . . . . . . . . . . . 32
Intimations of Mortality . . . . . . . . . . . . . . . . . . . 34
The Golden Flower . . . . . . . . . . . . . . . . . . . . . . 36
In the Kitchen (I) . . . . . . . . . . . . . . . . . . . . . . . 37
In the Kitchen (II) . . . . . . . . . . . . . . . . . . . . . . . 39
A Sestina for Mother Eve . . . . . . . . . . . . . . . . . . 41
Beginnings . . . . . . . . . . . . . . . . . . . . . . . . . . . . 43

## But Man, Proud Man

What Course after Nightfall? . . . . . . . . . . . . . . . . 49
If Men Loved Life . . . . . . . . . . . . . . . . . . . . . . . 51
World Sacrifice . . . . . . . . . . . . . . . . . . . . . . . . . 55
Strict Is the Charge . . . . . . . . . . . . . . . . . . . . . . 62

# *Foreword*

> *Forsan et haec olim meminisse iuvabit.*
> —Virgil's *Aeneid*, Bk I, 1.203

The poems in *Brief Authority* were all written after Rebecca Pitts retired on 1976 and are unified by an intellectual purpose that may be called autobiographical. She was always seeking to bring together her life and her work—to practice what she believed. She wanted to have a functional relationship to society—to express her concern in action. She was part of the rebellion of the thirties, but was always preoccupied with the broadest cultural issues—above all with her experience of finitude, one of the major themes of these poems, which seem to me to explore that experience from the point of view of a woman who has lived through the twentieth century and meditated upon what she has done and thought and felt. Her first essay, called "Something to Believe In," was published in *The New Masses* in the early 1930s. Another essay, "Prayer and the Incarnation," appeared in the *Hibbert Journal* (April 1953). For the first issue of *Womankind*, a local feminist periodical, she wrote "Are We 'Our Own Worst Enemies'?" These titles suggest her major interests—philosophy, theology, metaphysics, and politics—interests she pursued with passion throughout her life.

From her youth she wrote poetry, but one day she gathered all her poems together and burned them. Then she conceived the plan for *Brief Authority* as a series of autobiographical poems, which would reveal her vision of reality—not as a carefully constructed, logical system, but as a series of moments of insight in which her passion for truth would radiate and perhaps be remembered by others in the future with pleasure. With Horace, she believed that poetry is more lasting than bronze.

Indianapolis, Indiana,
August 17, 1985

Allegra Stewart

*Brief Authority*

# Theater

This theater is too large     too dark     for surgery
but the great still crowd no doubt has much to lose
and will never contemplate this frozen moment
as if it were merely another performance of one more play.

Under the fierce lights down there
the men in green masks must be surgeons.
But why is the knife arrested? why is it all so crucial and uncertain?
who is the covered quiet figure on that table?
and are the surgeons friendly?

Like a still frame from some experimental cinema
(its end not yet determined),
all this has the structure of vision
                      of nightmare and memory image—
it has the look of a poem fastened forever on the page
in itself arrested     meaningless     empty
               waiting to be completed
by anyone in the audience
               or by every reader
each one an unfinished interpretation
of the same invisible text.

# Program Note

My program may or may not come off
                          on Sunday however
the bank is open
                                the tellers are busy upstairs
telephones have to be used if the dark one is reached
if I remember
                        exactly how the push-lock worked
and escape down these stairs—it will not be easy—

this series has been presented on WISH
I myself prefer television
                        but the Negro has given me a set of fat tapes
something odd though has been added to the pie pans
It will soon be high time to ask if there is any meaning to all this
does the House in the Country ring any bells?
and why all the crisp green lettuce?

# Meditation

I cannot make Time stop, nor clearly see
what my dreams mean.     Yet I presume to know
what Time is for.     To know Eternity.

Where do dreams come from?     What is memory?
They enter Time, and out of Time they flow.
But can I make Time stop?     How can I see?

Meaning is purpose, wrapt in mystery.
Mere Time seems blind and tedious, blind and slow.
What is it for?     Who sees Eternity?

But at this moving point that seems to flee
we learn a little—here and there a clue:
Time freezes in those naves that make us see

how human aspiration climbs the sky;
or fluid in music's meaning whispers low
"I find my pattern in Eternity."

And bright leaves fall now from that bronzing tree,
taking the heart with beauty as they go.
Time will not stop for them, that's plain to see,

nor stay for us who linger, wistfully,
while red September berries fade.     And so
we cling to Time and want Eternity.

The bright fire fades, the coals die down, and we
are soon for bed indeed, but the late glow
has made Time seem to pause, and now I see
what Time is for.     To *mean* Eternity.

# The Dance

*Truth was their model as they strove to build
A world of lasting objects to believe in,
Without believing earthenware and legend,
Archway and song, were truthful or untruthful:
The Truth was there already to be true.*
—W. H. Auden

*For the man who loves God and his companion in one—though he remains in all the frailty of humanity—receives God for his companion.*
—Martin Buber

*But in dark weeping helpless moments of peace
Women and poets believe and resist forever:
The blind inventor finds the underground river.*
—Muriel Rukeyser

*Pain—and every real happening in the soul—is to be compared not with a drama but with those early mysteries whose meaning no one learns who does not himself join in the dance. . . . Only participation in the existence of living discloses the meaning in the ground of one's own being.*
—Martin Buber

*The cobra was known as the Eye . . . symbol of mystic insight and wisdom. . . . In pre-dynastic Egypt the female deity of lower Egypt (north) was the Cobra Goddess known as Ua Zit. Not a great deal is known about this most ancient Cobra Goddess, but we later see Her as the uraeus cobra worn upon the foreheads of other deities and Egyptian royalty. . . . Later derivations of the Cobra Goddess, such as Hathor and Maat, were both known as the Eye.*
—Merlin Stone

# Soliloquy

"Call in your heedless
thoughts and hone
an accurate scalpel
steel on stone
cut out the needless
stand alone.

"For Time is a river,"
cries the crone,
"flowing forever,
now here     now gone.
Lie down in silence
divest the bone."

"But Life is an eddy,"
her self sings in answer,
"breasting Time's current
as dancing and dancer
and never
                        alone

Sing the Companion
not yet known."

## Strangers

As two ships, tall masted,
with bellying white sails,
career in vivid solitude,
tacking western gales—
and over curved horizons
sighting each other's prow,
put out stiff, stately signals,
so "I," and "Thou."

How distant veer     those lonely sails
through the brightening dawn.
Foam-furrows following their trails
melt, and both are gone.

Sunset finds each—one silhouette—
stark on a copper sky.
But where is the lost message
veiled in that brief passage
through Eternity?

## On Calypso's Island

Clouded this isle whereon I roam
Trailing dim memories of home,
Hoping with aging eyes half blind     to mark
The dark path I must find.

Cypress and alder-thickets hide the sea
From me     who seek the tide,
Long-heard but never within reach,
For there's no pathway to the beach.

Clouded this island where I wander,
But when I climb that high hill yonder,
I catch a far-off gleam of sun on foam,
And home seems less a dream.

Odysseus, Homer tells us, here was bound
And found her kiss was dear
Who bedded him night after night
Though tears came back with each day's light.

No hero I, no heroine,
But I too watch Calypso spin—
Must fear her frail enchantment, weep the past
That cast me here on sleep.

How sweet her promises, how rare the gifts
She lifts before me there
Where her cave dazes my dim eyes
And magic takes me with surprise.

Crowded this isle, yet each alone
Goes there, no comrade can be known,
And when you eat and drink Calypso's cheer,
Fear what has passed your lips.

Calypso the concealer hides from me
The sea—hides all that's real.
But like all captives on this isle
I meet her mocking special smile.

Daughter of Providence, she hides
One buried stream that seaward glides,
Whose bubbling watergates might breathe, if heard
Some word     that liberates.

# A Dream of Meaning

Extending
to a far horizon
this sheet of water is sheer
satin      or mirror      yet broken
all round me by a great low-jutting oval
of irregular stone piles

I am descending
totally without fear
(though in waking life I am terrified of water)

Dimly translucent
                         growing more clear
as I go down      it seems      into light
the green-gold sea is not alien
to the sea's daughter

But I am enclosed by broken
pillars      by the blind arches of a sunken
a ruined inverted
Colosseum
and I seem to see with invincible clarity
how this dead oval enclosure
this gaping temenos
means only a spoiled eye
                   a colossal "I"
that oldest illusion
And the green-gold waters beckon
queer quiet distant words are spoken
"It stretches very far . . . all the way to 'ŏps' "
(this word rhymes with *stops*),
with lean economy driving home the point
fine as a needle at point of entry
                   yet like acupuncture
conveying no hurt
                   not even a warning sensation
though the needle's eye will broaden later to accept Your
measureless ironic Force

Imagine if you will the
self-assurance        pompous and almost coarse
relying on half-forgotten Latin
I laugh:      "Silly
there's no such word as *ŏps*
you must mean *ōps*"
(Now that word rhymes with *hopes*
and means power and wealth among other things
but has lost this nominative singular form in Latin
a fact I had forgotten)

But the odd little word
repeated with firm courtesy
implies that . . .
                well . . . if you insist . . .
your choice will do
                but *ŏps* was correctly heard
I wake up chuckling at the small "Latin" lesson
so smartly given—in sleep, too!—by the self-corrected learning
in a mere matter of thirty seconds or so
yet dimly aware that some forgotten Message
telescoped into one quick moment
                of far-gazing . . .
                      of ghostly hearing . . .
must be decoded
                and will never let me go.

# Sea Figure

*Allu mari mi portati*
*Se voleti chi mi sanati*

*Allu mari, allu via*
*Cosi m'ama la donna mia*
*Allu mari, allu mari. . . .*

—*Hymn sung by women refugees*
*from the Inquisition*

**1**

    Carry me to the Sea
    if you want me to be healed
    to the Sea, to the Way
    thus does my Lady love me
    to the Sea, to the Sea. . . .

For how many hundreds of thousands
was this hymn, in the Times of Burning,
a cry of glad passion, of greeting!
They came down to the white sea sands,
running to escape
vile torture, slander, rape,
destruction of spirit,
bright curl of smoke and flame about charred bone.
From every evil a woman can inherit
they fled, in their great yearning
for this embrace, this death, this meeting.
Singing, they plunged into the kind blue waters
to be received, they thought, like well-loved daughters,
or as lover by the beloved, each alone.

*Cosi m'ama la donna mia. . . .*
Thus does my Lady love me. . . .

But what was the Sea singing as she called them?
Oblivion—dark quiet end of sorrow?
Or in some cave of memory did they hear an echo
of a long war-cry down the ships at Naxos:
Come, "Mystics to the Sea"?      Was it a promise?
A cry of victory?

**2**
Beautiful, cruel, ambiguous as any oracle,
the sea is forever a symbol, and more than a symbol
she really has been what she says to us—the long memory of our cooled star.
But can she speak truly of purpose     of meaning     of intention?
She is varied, incredibly prodigal, blind to the death in her green caves—
spawning life, freezing her fossils, now and then tossing landward
some of her only partly successful odd creations
(is it chance or purpose tossing?     who knows?), and now they are
                                   strangely transmuted.
Source then of the vast genetic broth each gene encoded
with structural memory—yes—and maybe a partial purpose,
for each gene knows
the vital function of its parts each without pity
divides to repeat itself     intends to become immortal,
or dimly yearning for some deeper transaction
(if briefly in union with another of its kind
and merging identity with the other forever),
wills to make fleeting vehicles for its own survival,
seeming to serve, meanwhile, unknowing, a larger purpose—
the making of more intricate, less transient carriers of life.

**3**
*Seeming,* we say.     You cannot prove more than *seems.*
Ask, if you will, the ultimate question:
"Is there some final purpose in life—any point to creation
beyond our blind partial urges to go on living?"

But looking for cosmic purpose in rocks the sea laid down,
you are probably reading that record by the light of your own candle—
your limited ends, your fears, your partial human pride—
in any case bound to the vanishing horizontal
dimension of Time, in any case asking *Now,*
probing the changeable fleeting outer world
for the past you contain yourself and the purpose your Self must arrive at.

**4**
But from the Sea, from the sea-foam, from the great water
rises forever the Love Goddess in her splendor.
Or at Agra in early spring, Death having carried her under,
rises Earth's Savior and lost Self, Demeter's daughter.
Timeless renewals—timeless and strangely tender—
these mysteries: utter our birth from the Sea, but point to one later—
and greater.

On the shore, on the night shore, stumbling we trace
the grief-blinded Mother's dazed journey—at the last dark portal
dancing a veiled maze-dance.       For all who would see the fullness
or harvested truth at Eleusis must come to this place.
Shed then your lendings.       Cast off into the stillness
All that is mortal.
To the Sea, Mystics.       To the Sea.       "Mystics to the Sea!"

## 5
Mother and memory of all Life—and ours—
and known from of old as a fertile Mother Goddess
(called "Nammu" by the early Sumerians—
"Nammu, the mother who gave birth to earth and heaven"—
a Name they wrote with the ideogram for "sea"),
but more than a mother,
the Sea is literal type or *figura* of all our varied arrivals,
of every new advent, every partial fulfilment.

Image of latent Mind creating Life in the waters,
image of limitless possibility
for Life on this planet       perhaps on a myriad others,
she is pointing forever toward Mind and its inner oceanic spaces.

## Song for a Voyager

There is one journey and one journey only
that's worth your time to go,
whether by jet or liner or slow freighter.
If you leave where you are, the way you travel
leads to those inner spaces, sooner or later,
as you will come to know.
There's but one journey, and one journey only.

Admire if you will at Notre Dame the portal,
at Chartres the great rose window.
Have you discovered yet the Queen of Heaven?
Not a pale Virgin simpering at her son,
but the august, immortal
figure of wisdom, power, and splendor?

Or in dark glasses on the sands at Giza
have you seen clear the massive
implacable features of the superhuman,
ruling a beast, impassive?
She waits our end with her undying question
from woman back to woman.

No sand,      no city, holds your destination:
seek only the Bright Stranger
hidden within your sole, your single fate.
Remember now, the wind-tossed Sea is lonely—
the long way filled with danger.
Then touch with awe the horns of consecration.
Departing, kneel at the Horn Gate.
For there's one journey, and one journey only.

# The Horn Gate

Yet beware, voyager.     You cannot find
that radiant Stranger in such emptiness
as yawns within you.     Probe your "deeper mind":
explore your dreams.     Through all that nothingness
you'll sluice some fascination, perhaps terror:
dramas in Technicolor;     grinning faces;
dim hideous beasts; forms, words, that come to mirror
shards of your life unlived     or lived in places
better forgot than lingered in. These traces—
all corpsed—must be ejected from deep slime
and looked at. They're what's yours.     (For the far sea-spaces
of Mind, true Mind—these are not yours.)     In time
you'll cry, "This dark thing is mine own."     But there—
where you touch ruin—lies medicine for despair.

**1**
Surely the old masters of memory and song
were at least partly wrong.
Is there ever an Ivory Gate?
They meant, those poet-sages, that now and then a sleeper
may snatch through the Gate of Horn some revelation—
Some truth dredged from the past, or a glimpse of someone's fate.
But through the ivory portal, so they said,
flit the false fleeting shades of acts long dead,
jumbled with meaningless fears and hopes, echoes of ignorant strife.
Well, I'd hate to say each splinter
of wish or memory
out of my personal history
is worthy of prolonged examination,
though even these faded fragments may well mirror
some truth—and drift of my sleepwalking life.
But when it comes to nightmare, or in the recurrent terror—
the white waste desolation
of the world's winter,
vistas of endless desert sands,
the walled-up corpse, the conspirators' ghastly error,
the class that was cut all term, the failed examination,
the blasted Tree, and the rape beneath the Tree
(God! that Old Man with horrible hands!)
then I'd say to the sleeper:

"Dig deeper.
Remember the face that's reversed in every mirror;
remember the mirage—it is never, and always, there
(often the traveler sees it upside down),
but far from that false oasis, that towered town,
lies a real place somewhere."

## 2

Then I'd go on to say:
"Think how this ship—your own particular Way—
cuts through a perilous night sea.
So whenever you, as pilot, seek to embark,
stand watch at once when you've set sail
and wait for the naked stranger with a message,
who'll glide up, phosphor-gleaming, white as a shark,
climb your neglected ladder, drip on your deck,
naked, need clothing (furnished without fail
from your soiled store), then beg a fugitive's passage.
Dressed in your togs—the dirty residue
of a life's stiff gestures, habits, crimes against light—
this guest looks like your shadow, your defiled soul-image,
and comes from a ship that's called "your destiny,"
"your burden," or "your course." But the shape is never you:
there's purpose here that's firmer, sterner than your slight
sleepwalking drift through day as well as night;
and the tale that's told is strange (it may be savage),
having no foothold in your memory.

## Prisoner

This is a white dead lunar landscape
black, though, with a shaft of night
                        where a tall tower lifts
and I think I must be dreaming about Babel
or some triumph of twentieth-century technology
male mastery and nuclear know-how
it is not steam however
                        that hisses from this arrogant column
a song of sibilant sorrow
I listen with pity but without terror
with pity and rage for an Ancient One
for the Great Snake reared high in Her encircling prison

## Cobra Goddess

The slow curve of the ballerina's leap
                          the fall of ripeness
How fatally easy to say "Our Father"
                          but suddenly the stillness
is lit with a woman's hooded figure and a cobra
leaps to her pointing finger
hooded and lovely
they burn against dark in a denying image
O Mother        Mother
                          no sounding
of harmony brings truth
                          exactitude of analysis
does not disclose it
                          the color fades
but never in all these autumns
                          that red-gold question

# Setting Out

What piles          what long          deserted pier
what water lapping softly
and far across sand an old gray hostel
strange yet familiar in the fading sunset
the scent of scrub pine dying on dusky air
blent with faint odors of fish and wave. . . .

At this still moment before the tide turns outward
I have cast off          to rock          to linger here
in an old creaky boat          its ribbed inverted nave
beaten by sand and surf          unused          beyond repair.
It was given me long ago          but I had forgotten
the rusty oar-locks          the cracked oars          the battered sides
now to be given helpless to the tides. . . .

Up over my shoulder in the pale green sky
the first stars glimmer          but what is this other Light
star and no star          now brilliant and then dimmer
now near          now all too far
can I move toward it through the coming night
in this old boat          this leaky          this half-rotten?

It is the tide that moves me          gently          with no returning
it is resistless          see how its long low swell
pulls through the marching darkness toward the open sea
these floating weeds the bobbing refuse of this shore
and with slow gathering force my crippled boat and me
I hardly breathe          I do not lift an oar
while over east-moving waters a distant bell
tolls a grave warning. . . .

And yet . . . and yet . . .
what tide is this          what course          just now the pier
was empty and distant as any grief-stunned heart
determined to forget
now it draws strangely near
and half-familiar figures over the waters
summon me there . . . whose face . . . whose lips that seem to part
now changeable          now more clear
who are these others
sisters I loved or never knew          my mother          my foremothers
and O my lost          my own          my unborn daughters. . . .

Last look at memory
first glimpse of unborn time beyond this hour
or somehow both—as if the vast heart of the sea
merged in one beat systole and diastole,
and time, curved back into eternity,
burst into flower?

It cannot matter     nothing is now required
but full surrender to this great strange tide
and the eastward light that beckons     though in the west
with grace of awakened sense it seems
dear Life quickens and redeems
moments long lost     wild strawberries tasted on a summer hill
or a moonlit meadow circled with dark trees:
Nothing must be desired
not even such things transfigured—nothing denied
not even all bleak uncomprehended ill
not even the slime where life was so long mired—
for against that reef thunders the strong ebb tide
and beyond those straits roll mightier waves than these.

# Advent and Eleusis
*For Muriel Rukeyser*
*December 15, 1913–February 12, 1980*

We gather together one darkening afternoon
an almost coven of innocent white witches
to welcome a coming birth.    As it happens    the day
is Advent Sunday in 'Seventy-nine, but nobody mentions it
not even the one-time Catholics in our midst
who might have remembered.
                     Wine flows, gifts are assembled
soft blankets    Pampers    bootees    and knitted jackets
all that a baby will need    for we love the expectant mother
whose bittersweet wit and comic dislike of men
so often delight our meetings.
                     On this day we have chosen
to speak of the world "according to Garp" and the
absurd    the almost virgin birth    the misgbegotten adventures
and meaningless death    of that amiable hero.
I will remember that day.    It was Advent Sunday
pointing to Birth    pointing to Death    that is woven
over the warp of the world's loom.
                     Allegra comes late
white-faced and strained    and we feel the coming shadow—
an absurd nursing-home accident    an aging sister's
hip broken    and three weeks later at Christmas
life-hope and sorrow meet in the porch of Death
as pregnant Josie (almost unable to come)
attends the last service for Allegra's sister
Lucille    frustrate so long    and worn by pain
who has slipped away gently in silence toward a deeper silence.

"Was it a birth or a death?"    So Eliot's Magus
touching this matter of putting on human flesh
and laying it down.    A question no longer his
(not even, if I may venture to say it, "His")
it is ours    who might also welcome another birth
(and another death) if we met them.

Being "just a Jew," as you put it, who "believed in Jesus,"
you never phoned me on Christmas    it was always *my* birthday
(I too was an Advent child.) Last year you didn't    the snow fell softly.

Christmas Eve comes     death waits     a small birth is expected.
("Rejoice," writes Josie later, "beyond a common joy.")
You and I speak across years and coming death and distance.
Love has no body     I can find no Word
to gather all your ages in one clasp.

The long Year turns     another Advent has gone     and you,
who lived your life and wrote your poems for freedom
and the passion that is peace
("I want to break open," you cried once, knowing so deeply
what shell must be broken in birth that is also death),
have entered death's silence on a day of birth
still cherished a little by a forgetful nation.
Loving that nation as Lincoln loved it
you mourned its grievous failures,
raged at its corporate crimes,     with bitter wit
mocked its mendacity,
dreaded the advent of its doom,     yet dreaming deliverance
tried to invent or reveal the "underground river"
deep-flowing beneath all false desires—that dream
which "women and poets," you thought, "believe . . . forever."

But though born at the Year's end     in mid-December
you never mentioned "Advent."
Nor spoke of Eleusis, antique city of Birth
(sacred, they say, to a great Birth-Goddess):
city whose very name
is Greek for *Advent*—a child's arrival—
site of those Greater Mysteries, women's mysteries
where the ripe soul's going was celebrated
in a silent reaping of late autumn grain.

Yes, you were silent about these mysteries.
All your poems, however,
celebrate mystery:
sing birth     sing the glad running of children
sing the true grace     the meaning     the depth of promise in women
sing above all the arrival of new meanings
and the burst of Light when the quick Spirit comes.

Were you always      so mute about Advent and Eleusis
because of an arcane promise in that hushed harvesting—
a timeless hope hidden in Bethlehem's stable—
were they a little too bright
too rich in their still symbols of resurrection
for our death-darkened planet?

No, this would not have been like you
who knew betrayal      felt coming death      thirsted for joy
sang joy out of suffering.
You had known waking      healing      and holy Light
long      long      before leaving us.
                            And now . . .
now in this darkening late afternoon
of a sick planet's history . . .
now . . . as everywhere women are mourning those whom death has harvested
or will soon harvest . . . now as women are singing
glad in the advent of new life they have welcomed . . .
now . . . now . . . is the time for the unlocked heart      the unsealed
     eye . . .
now, as we hear rich music from your heart broken open
in Love.      Love for the world . . . for all that truly lives.
It waits in your poems      just as you told us . . .
Love out of silence.

## Star

A faint star looked at straight will disappear,
as children know. "Tell truth," said Emily,
"but tell it slant." That clear-cut melody
is not the music's meaning.　　When you hear
meaning,　　it makes a murmurous underflow
half heard at hearing's border.　　So with mind:
on target, empty; or if not, confined
within strict walls of what it wants to know;
but wait—look elsewhere—quiet—then you'll mark,
strayed from some corner of your inner knowing,
visiting strangers, voices soft and far,
and images like jewels in the dark—
bringing you news of how Time's wind is blowing,
and the face of love, where all the meanings are.

# The World in Our Heart

*Everything has been made beautiful in its time; also the world has been set in their heart; therefore no one can search out the work that has been done from the beginning to the end.*
—Ecclesiastes 3:11

*The kitchen is the place of creative change.*
—C. G. Jung

*The heavens declare the glory of God; and the firmament showeth His handywork. Day unto day uttereth speech and night unto night showeth knowledge. There is no speech or language where their voice is not heard.*
—Psalm 19:1–3

*Though there is but one Center, most men live in Centers of their own.*
—Heraclitus (paraphrased)

*The spirit is inserted in sparks into the life of all; it bursts out into flame in the life of the most living . . . and from time to time there burns somewhere a great fire of the spirit.*
—Martin Buber

*For their sakes I consecrate myself.*
—John 18:19

*Revelation means the moment in which we are surprised by the knowledge of someone there in the darkness and the void of human life; it means the self-disclosure of light in our darkness. . . . When we speak of revelation we mean that moment when we are given a new faith, to cleave to and to betray, and a new standard, to follow and deny.*
—H. Richard Niebuhr

## On the Beach

They billow        and loiter        rapidly        like blown leaves
before a gust of joy.        More silent than leaves, however
(their skates are padded):        on the cement of this long "boardwalk"
any metallic hum would utterly
drown the tide's voices.
The tan bodies of young athletes
are riding the surf.        Is joy the secret?
Bicycles glide by slow and silent        young faces are flushed
with happiness or a brisk breeze.

Sunlight is brilliant
on the bright blue Pacific.
Halfway across the horizon
a tall white wave is breaking        topples its foam
crawls forward with surging fingers
while to the left we feel the slow-gathering swell
of another breaker.

We stop to chat with a skater who is laughing
and breathless—she has just picked herself up.
"These skates," she hisses in a German voice,
"they are really goot for nussing—really, they spread this vay"—
making a V with her splayed fingers.

"Everything beautiful in its time."        Now is a time
for joy.        It is easy to take such a world into your heart.

                                          San Diego, November 1, 1981

## Hieroglyphics

Hand on the waist-high cement parapet,
I look down at the damp sand of the beach,
smooth as cement, and tan
where the evening tide has swept it—
marked, however, with morning hieroglyphics:
the pronged track of the gull's foot,
stars left by the pigeons,
the tiny asterisks of sandpipers.

Soon now the incoming tide
will creep to this parapet
and then, receding,
leave the sand bare and featureless.

Hieroglyphics.    Antique, half-holy word.
These prints do not really look Egyptian
but I think of the Pharaohs,
whose long almost inscrutable inscriptions
say only: "We were here.    Authority was ours."

I think also of their late successor
whose violent death invaded our living rooms
in early October.

Good man (it may be even great), his
sense of the tides of history
seemed unique among so many foolish figures
in this impoverished age.

Mourned officially for many reasons
(few of them genuine, or good),
Sadat lies hidden in the sands he loved—
and in our fragile memories
who wept for ourselves in his going.

Small wonder that half the world
for a few days sorrowed together,
made one in fear and grieving.
And everywhere we failed to fathom
the mystery of this working—
that the one in our time most needed
was the one swept away by tides of hatred.

What does it "mean," if anything,
that with only one man's death
the broken world was set, but oh, so briefly,
in so many hearts?

                San Diego, November 2, 1981

## Hunter Moon

A shivering windswept late afternoon
and late leaves falling
someone is burning a pile of them in the distance
the faint sharp smell of smoke brings memories of childhood.

We keep on stuffing old leaves into trash bags
another gust and we rake again
it is all to do over
(backs aching . . . strain in the muscles).

It is a useless necessary harvest
year after year     this clearing away
of what once lived     yet beneath brown death
bright grass is still alive     still burns with green.

The wind is dying.     We'll have another
frost tonight.     Each morning for a week
I have looked out to see silver
dust glinting on blades of grass     they were all separate
small bayonets.

It is almost quiet now in the evening garden
where only a few dead chrysanthemums
still rustle on their stalks.

I look up at nameless yet familiar constellations
in pale gray city sky.
Bright moonlight shines on one withered red chrysanthemum
its silver brilliance making the grass look frosty.

The moon sails full and slow from the west
a great gold chrysanthemum     a "Golden Flower"
full-blown in the place of Heaven.

I want to say "Harvest Moon" but November
belongs to the "Hunter."

And I remember the baying of hounds in
wooded hills to the south        the staccato barking of guns
where Our Lady of the Wild Things
brings only death with her radiance.
Death to the small, the friendless,
the raccoons and possums.

And I know my country is
scarred and blistered with nuclear installations,
Diablo Canyons and Three Mile Islands
(silos of packed disaster, no promise of plenty),
that the Western desert is overrun with
emplacements of death, steel hounds ready to spring.

The world's body is already sick and broken.
What can moonlight mean to these hunters—
its silver gleaming on barbed wires, on the helmets of sentries,
on bayonets?

                                    Indianapolis, Mid-November 1981

# Intimations of Mortality

*(Children at the Horn Gate)*

**1**
I knew too well one violent small child
and wild.
She was only three or four
when she'd beat her doll's brass head
savagely on the splintered old kitchen floor.
To enlarge the holes?   To make the hard thing "dead"?
She never said,
but hating the live brassy stare,
wanted to push it into the dark down there—
that emblem of what threatened and confined
her small unhappy mind.

**2**
This child lacked speech to tell her fears by daylight:
the wild noon panic in a dizzying sun,
the horrible transformations in the twilight
of stair-post, rocking chair, library table
(how late the gas lamps were turned on!).

All children fight such fears if they are able,
but terror is sometimes worse.
Into this little haunted house of life,
with all the power of a prenatal curse
wound sinister echoes of an ancient horn
(even to see a horn brought panic strife,
so Mother threatened to blow it whenever she had to warn).

And pitched dark past all other common fears—
that steel-mill Satan murking in furnace fires,
with spiral horns, with half-beast eyes and ears.

Smooth to explain the forms these terrors took,
but how explain the shudder, the numb trance
with power to choke and freeze such innocence—
this energy yet untouched by "bad" desires,
this mind still unprepared to look
at one page of life's book?

**3**
It is the fear, the fear itself that cries
for light.    Most children shudder so, no doubt—
though many soon forget.    If not,
like this one, they will question the dumb skies
why terror must take the blameless by surprise.

She was loved, this child, and knew it.    Why then was night
so often strangled by still deeper fright?
Poor small strange-starred somnambulist,
seemingly by disaster early kissed—
and driven in sleep to the soft, comforting light
of Mother's room, screaming and wordless—why
(lifted and warmed and hugged) could she not tell
what images had plunged her toward such hell,
nor even remember the horror of her cry?

## The Golden Flower

Homeless and tentless in their painted meadow,
they mistook dusk for dawn, sought the great Flower
of self-fulfillment, found only its faint shadow—

knew the Ten Thousand Things were thin as air
yet hoped to evoke from dust and aspiration
an immortal body, a radiance, their desire.

Though within nowhere lay their native nation,
how safe they felt!     Reality seemed their home—
kind Void and clear, waiting their recognition.

But, House of the Real, you're crumbled, not the same,
we can no longer paint you, form a world image
for sense or spirit, call the "real" by its Name,

seeing ten thousand mysteries work to ravage
minds that probe flux for form, for permanence,
both wanting.     Now this monstrous empty cleavage—

while the world aches like toothache with such absence.
Moon just a cold stone, not the Golden Flower
(her eclipse recorded on a plate, for sense

to gape at).     Lonely one, it's not the hour
for Chinese yoga.     Still, wisdom makes you wince:
who walk their way alone, themselves devour.

# In the Kitchen (I)

**1**
Strange—how the pundits and shamans of every period
have dared to proclaim the destiny—the doom—of women.
"Kitchen . . . the place of creative change." Thus the great medicine-man
                        of our century—
serene on his height, secure above the cluttered cupboards,
the kettle that nearly boils over into the quiet madness, the
greasy stacks of dishes, the whining children, the creaky pump,
the stopped-up drain, the vista of monotonous days
destined to lengthen, with their back-breaking burden of
stooping over a soiled sink, into the heart-breaking
funeral of the future.

Having pored earnestly over his loved alchemical texts,
Jung has surmised that the retorts of Paracelsus
must have boiled over now and then
and that Melchior, for his homunculus, must have concocted very often
a greasier mixture than your scant stews—my worn-out, my long-
                        buried mother,
and you, my unknown sisters, still buried deep below the poverty line.
But believing that "man," eager in his perpetual quest for
infinity—that white transforming stone—
and projecting, meanwhile his strange passion onto many unpalatable items—
sought to transmute his leaden nature, and the world's, into the
                        gold of Heaven,
"Here is an archetype!" cries Dr. Jung.
For there, in the alchemist's kitchen—
that long solitude of useless, repetitive cooking—
he has found, he thinks, a perfect image for the endless work of self-creation.

**2**
But have you not seen O shaman, have you never counted
those bitter, hysterical housewives, bitten with intolerable boredom
(not many poor, but all—like their gaunt stricken sisters—
stripped of a great birthright, and for the same mess of pottage,
no matter who cooked it, well or ill);
have you never tried to count them, in your clinic—
those women who fled to you, helpless, dreaming (or screaming) of kitchens?
And in kind, authoritative accents have you not told them
(here are your very words):

> She [woman] can do everything [and *must?*] for love of a man.
> But those women who can achieve something important for the love
> of a thing are most exceptional, for this does not really agree
> with their nature

And haven't you sent them back to their cramped domestic finitude,
heartened, they thought, by its     implied importance,
its beautiful agreement with their "nature"?

I think of one nineteenth-century would-be Moses,
who broke his vows to Regina, renounced his promised marriage,
since *woman, he thought, stands quite differently from man,
in a dangerous rapport to finitude.*
Kierkegaard would have agreed with you, dear venerable Doctor,
in your odd views     of women. You have both regarded us only
in this one "essential" (that is to say, this wholly in accord with our "nature,"
but to you how convenient, how useful!) role—
this cozy rapport with finitude.
We know who has cooked your dinner and washed your dishes.

It is indeed dangerous, this rapport—and real.
For it bears our weakness and our real destiny.
Danger all women stand in—yes—but it's hardly the
"finite" in itself that makes the danger.
Whom does it frighten with its small shadow?
And you, who thought the alchemists' toil important—
who praised them for braying the tiny     and often the repulsive
in the mortar of endless search in the mire of matter—
be honest now, Dr. Jung, what were those fellows really seeking?
Was the "finite" they looked for worthy of endless devotion?
Was it really important? And why was their work so futile?

## In the Kitchen (II)

But Mother, it's still your kitchen I am sitting in. Mother (you for whom
my own life bore such an early weight of sorrow
that I hardly mourned your going), you still impart to me
the frail occasional fragrance of some present Being,
and first for you I would praise finitude.

I know your monotonous moments must have lengthened
to a sense of the endless!         To end in pain.
But they were far more, those moments, than any mere link in a sequence
from past to future—as your life was so much more
than a mere link from your foremothers to your rebel daughter
and the departed son, whose star rose splendid
in the story of his science.
So for you, my mother, for you first, for *you,*
I would praise finitude.

This is still your kitchen.
The old cramped space is here, the same old broken pump,
but the outer and inner scenes are modernized a little.
They are overfed cats, not children, who whine and tease amid their saucers.

Your kitchen was always in order, but my kitchen table is
cluttered with vitamins, books, and feminist papers—
with pamphlets on rape, on toxic waste, on countless endangered species—
not ever laid neatly for that early delectable dinner
you were always hurrying home to set before a heedless husband
who gulped it and never noticed.
                It was your daughter, of course,
who saw the small cup of pansies or nasturtiums,
who tasted and praised the flaky crusts, the
succulent round steak (old-fashioned, fried in flour, like chicken),
the creamy new peas and potatoes.
                It was your daughter, later,
who read through her homesick tears your simple weekly letters:

My dear Rebecca,

Monday was washday so I did the downstairs curtains, too. Tuesday I gave
Nicky a bath. He didn't like it, but he purred afterward. And you ought to have

seen how he helped me entertain the WCTU on Wednesday. He stood at the door and said good-bye to every one of the ladies. They thought he was beautiful, with his great plumy yellow tail!

The Bertha Ballard Board met yesterday. I couldn't stay for the tea and cookies because Dad's supper has to be so early, but Mrs. F. tells me that part was very nice. But we voted to raise the room and board for the girls to eight dollars a week. I thought that was too bad.

We had fried chicken and green beans and mashed potatoes for supper tonight, with tomatoes right out of the garden. I wish you could have had some. I miss you.

Two weeks and it will be Yearly Meeting time at Plainfield. I hope Dad won't be too busy to drive over, at least on Sunday. The bus fare is too much. I think I have enough saved in the cracker jar, though, to get there on Saturday.

Did I tell you I went to Dr. M. last week? He says my cataracts are getting much worse. I don't know how much longer I can be recording clerk of the Monthly Meeting. It has meant so much to me.

Your loving Mother

Mother, I know you loved my father,
but it wasn't for him—or not for him alone—
you could do "everything."     *Had* to do everything.
In those late years of quiet accepting—of loneliness and well-doing—
of weeping and missing your departed children—
it wasn't for him, or for us, you planted phlox and peonies,
trained roses to climb the kitchen porch, fed redbirds and sparrows,
hung on your clothesline a tiny home for the wrens,
who sometimes perched there between your very fingers.

Not only for him, nor for us,     your far-away children.

# A Sestina for Mother Eve

That mythic tale is not wholly false, nor wholly cruel to woman—
it was those arrogant, bearded redactors (they loathed every kind of new creation)
whose hate-poisoned pens (I intend this pun) shot sadism into the story.
For Light was there, and the visiting Eye; and the Voice—which *is* always—
                was there,
whispering into the ear of Its listening daughter
certain deep truths embedded in this fable of our history.

It was "Eve" did it, of course.      She led humankind into history
out of cold speechless caves.      For being a woman,
she was receptive to rumor and heard the Voice; and being Its daughter,
she was linked to Its pregnant silence and hushed promise of creation.
So when clumsy "Adam" lurched into the cave and swung his new fire-stick there
in the hollow half-dark, she foresaw the whole terrible story,
dimly foresaw it all, and accepted.      (There was no apple—that is a false,
                late story.)
What she did first was simple.      The hearth is the focus of history,
and even poor "Adam" could see it was warmer and brighter there,
though he wanted only to warm his hands.      But you see, it was first the
    woman
who stared at the flame and brooded, whose "third Eye" opened and saw creation,
not as more cubs and mere cooking; but, being Creation's daughter,
and seeing new forms and possible meanings, and seeing the birth of a great
                new Daughter
(whom we call "Truth," while we doubt her), "Eve" cried the first Word of
                Truth's story—
cried out in maternal pain and the painful joy of creation.
Here's the first Fall of our race—its Fall into speech and history—
that first clear numinous syllable, brought out of Light by a woman.
"But where were the Trees?" you are asking.      Of course.      They were
    there.

Or, rather, that Word was *the Knowledge-Tree's* root, though the Lie was also
                there—
Worm cutting the root of speech, slicing for use what Light's daughter
had seen at the world's heart.      And the *Tree of real Life* was first tasted
                by woman:
flame from a sky-flash kindled in her the core of our story,
though the long incredible horror of human history
has managed to veil its true greatness, the Inner Light of creation.

"And the serpent?" Well, snakes come later. Those earth-bound
    angels of
                    creation—
don't call them "phallic" symbols—much later they were sent there,
vessels of sacred venom, to sting into visions of history
antique oracular sibyls. They invited the Eye, they evoked once more the
                  old story,
told by new voices, in different words new-minted by each new daughter.
But by then the great powers of poet and priest had been brutally torn
                  from woman.
Her shrines were defiled, her story defaced, near-smothered in dust her torch
                  of creation.
Prone in the refuse of warlike power now lies Creation's daughter. And there—
there—look for Stanton's "true woman," that "dream of the future,"
                  and/or the End of all history.

# Beginnings

Writing is great and its beginning
a strange mystery.
But mark this:      a greater, a stranger mystery—
the speaking voice      the spoken word      the human glance.
Uncounted millennia before written history
people faced one another with true speech—
not with mere cries and grunts
or groans torn from half-human throats,
though kin to each
of these as to the scream of gull
rumble of great cat      howl
of wolf pack      hoot of owl.

With articulate symbol-bearing tone
humanity itself emerged      to reach
past momentary danger and ecstasy
or dumb organic loyalty
toward that which lies beyond in space      in time
alone
among earth's creatures able to name
not only spearheads      holy beasts      and flame
on altar-stone
but acts      thoughts      praise and blame
measure and coil of dance
red-brown ochre      great blaze of autumn tree
yesterday and tomorrow
love and sorrow.

Linguists are loathe to tell us of beginnings—
not so the mystics      not so the men of science.
"In the beginning . . . Word."      Or,      "In the beginning"—
that no-place of fires

where Space begins with the spiraling whirl of nebulae;
that "time" not in Time when Time begins with an Action
(For Time is Action): Space-Time a twin blaze out of some black Zero
state of potential;

and that same "time" when Mind begins (Mind the real Action?)—not manifest
    at first
where it sleeps quiet in the predictable motions
of matter in masses       the tracks of galaxies and stars
but leaping awake

implacably active in the sudden leap of quanta
creating new miracles of chemical transformation—
till with the dim and many million aeons
emerges an Ocean

on at least one planet.

Life leaps into being.

Then always that new more intricate       that strange surprise
in metamorphoses of genetic change and fading
is the leap of Mind—Mind building the Eye in new species
to greet the bright Sun,
Mind building the animal       Ear for warning and mating—making fin
    wing     and paw
to meet new challenge with old forms made over and transmuted—
but winning or losing, reshaping, discarding, creating or forgetting,
never predictable.

Call it chance if you must, or Time, or if you will, purpose,
but it had to be Mind:       Mind latent, potential—
in the brain, yes, but also in atom, in gene,
in the locked-in silent sleep of stone       in the prophet's voice—
as fire is potential

awaiting implosion under coercive stress.
And as every beast is driven to pasture with blows
Mind works at war with itself, since the blows and the beast
and the beast's reluctant stumble toward the pasture
all manifest Mind.

But on tongues of fire came the gift of speech that made us human.
Fire-fearers, fire-stealers, and in the end fire-makers,
we have painted in multiform myths of Promethean god or goddess
our real beginning

where bright twin branches of Mind's candelabrum—
perception of Fire's possible meaning and a true first Word
to show it to one another—were kindled together
in a chance moment,
whether here or there, in forest, in cave, or on grassland
matters no whit          perhaps at many places
but always, though Time and Fire were the spill, the point of contact,
it was new Mind that was kindled,
and Mind was the kindler.

# But Man, Proud Man

*Time past and time future*
*What might have been and what has been*
*Point to one end, which is always present.*
—T. S. Eliot


*We must admire in man the form of the formless, the concentration of the vast, the house of reason, the cave of memory.*
—Emerson


*Every beast is driven to pasture with blows.*
—Heraclitus


*Our planet that gets smaller every year . . . is in a process characterized by a refusal to remember. . . . We are surrounded by fictions about the past, contrary to common sense and an elementary perception of good and evil. . . . If such insanity is possible, is a complete loss of memory as a permanent state of mind improbable? Wouldn't that be worse than genetic engineering or the poisoning of our natural environment?*
—Czeslaw Milosz
(1980 Nobel lecture)


*The eye of a nihilist is unfaithful to his memories; it allows them to drop, to lose their leaves. . . . And what he does not do for himself he also does not do for the whole past of mankind: he lets it drop.*
—Nietzsche


*To be assaulted by the presence of greatness is not to take it in: a mountain makes no immediate impression of vastness—it conspires with the illusion of distance to conceal its proportions; and we only know them through the journey and the climb.*
—W. E. Hocking


*That which has been is now; and that which is to be has already been; and the Spirit requires of us that which is past.*
—Ecclesiastes 3:15

## What Course after Nightfall?

Came in the wild-red        fruitfall of the mid–twentieth century
seeing fire      seeing wings of terror      hearing the dead patrol
a poet, crying in the blackened ruins
"In my beginning is my end"—
meaning of course the purpose latent in every action,
meaning too the literal terminus of his English journey
to the site where his line was founded      an empty ancestral house
with a family motto shaking on a tattered curtain
as twilight gathered—but hinting a wider thought,
darker, more sinister, in that ravaged season:
that as an acorn holds the giant oak
so the dim past of human origins
has somehow contained and determined the whole course
of human destiny      to this end.

Yet "Time is a child," as Heraclitus said,
"playing at draughts—the kingly power is a child's."
                            So the game is always
an unskilled play of chance.      Each cast of dice
has an unpredictable outcome.      Here is no contradiction.
Probability rules      not fate      for modern science
although ten billion throws of dice
may make the end look certain and predestined
there is in every moment of time that one chance hovering—
the statistically improbable configuration.
And on this one chance      often-repeated
hangs our whole incredible history—
a story of life's appearance
                        of change      of novelty
new species emerging only to vanish
pinched out of existence in a straitened corner—
a record written in ancient rocks
(mind-prints of what indifferent Mind?).

Therefore as Darwin once saw clearly
humanity itself was never unavoidable
was never essential to Nature's multiple ends,
at least if no world intention is latent in all this—
no Divine End
masking its purposive actions as pure chance.
Which Divine End, as a matter of fact,
might well not include humanity as we know it
might well require our total change (perhaps our total destruction)
in fires of our own making.

It is twilight now     in a dim half-ruined house a
tired child is rolling dice against himself.

This is not dawn     day is not breaking:
men's goals point madly backward and
we are for the night.
Down memory's corridor sounds the voice of a great poet:
"What course after nightfall," cries a man called Pindar,
"has destiny written that we must run to the end?"
" . . . is our end"     rockets     stark fear     cities in terror and flight
white blaze     mushroom cloud     the world's funeral pyre?

"In our beginning . . . "     Light?     or Fire?

# If Men Loved Life

*In memory of Charles Preston—*
*who did love life*

> *Let the reformers descend from the stands where they are forever bawling!*
> *let an idiot or insane person appear on each of the stands!*
> *Let the Asiatic, the African, the European, the American, and the*
> *Australian go armed against the murderous stealthiness of each*
> *other! let them sleep armed! let none believe in good will!*
> *Let there be no unfathomable wisdom! let such be scorn'd and derided*
> *off from the earth! . . .*
> *Let all the men of These States stand aside for a few smouchers! let*
> *the few seize on that they choose! let the rest gawk, giggle, starve,*
> *obey!*
> —Walt Whitman

**1**

And now man's dearest dream
(I mean of uniting the human world by conquering Nature)—
that dream
under whose glare the pure headwaters of the Colorado
burst free from their high Rocky peaks and melting snow
to be chained and depleted on a long majestic journey
and enter the Gulf at last a barren brackish trickle;
that vision of limitless power to be drained from the mighty Columbia,
beloved of salmon and steelhead—and those Indian fishers
who alone would harvest them wisely—all this fades now into apprehension,
as the salmon are ravaged by loggers, poachers, and pollutants;
and power gasps a warning of coming failure; and the polluted water table—
everywhere. East and West—is falling—falling;
while a chemical dump in Indiana makes poison rain
over Canadian orchards. Here is our human world
united indeed—one splendid complexity of conquest and dying—
penultimate triumph of sterile reason and either-or logic.
Good servant of worthy ends, but a sinister master,
such reason powers now on a deep buried wish of the forgetful
who are only for themselves—under whose heedless hands
the last World Teacher of technical man (his blind, mechanical Messiah)
plods on—at incredible speeds, to be sure, but plodding and mindlessly pointing
only to mastery of means, but not—not to that hidden end.

## 2

It is perfectly plain, as one great woman puts it:
"If men loved life this planet would be different."
She was speaking, and so am I, not of all human males
(for here and there they are beautifully other in their insight):
she meant the dominant type in any either-or culture
(which is to say, in *every* patriarchal culture)—
where to win means always to pulverize an enemy,
to master means someone or something held in subjection,
and social order and rational thought seem always to demand
a stern repression—of others, yes, but also of the "Other"—
that "Bright Stranger, the foreign self," the subtle gentle wisdom
trying forever to shine through chinks in the mind's wall.

Here, then, is the man who observes, makes ruthless use of,
the beings he encounters,
who never goes out in soul and deed to meet them
with humble awareness of their right to be real,
or a simple exchange of gifts.

Here is a man looks into the pool of Nature
to find there a dim ballet of shadowy abstractions
or merely an angry ape.     He looks at a woman
to glory in her submission.     He struts when she flatters him.
One way or another he always enjoys her fear.

This man is preparing now the fate of fortress America
to challenge for rule over cities of the faceless dead
our mightiest mirror-image.     His solemn gabble, however
("strike power," "retaliation," "five-percent survival"),
holds not one syllable of grief for the forgotten dance of living.

This is the man we train little boys to imitate—
whose bodily swagger and stance of heart that dull perennial Boy
(learned or empty-headed, mass man of the millennia)
copies as he can.

If men—such men—loved life, our stricken planet
might still take heart, might live again, be whole
with a new holiness beyond our dreaming.
A terrible justice, however,
transforms an individual folly
into the madness of a mass desire.

I think they are all half-consciously in love with death—
envy its power, kill beasts for the joy of killing—
desire extinction even for themselves.
(Death only, you see, has the absolute dominion.)

**3**
Oh, wish I could mourn the Fall of Man as an eternal given
and wring my hands over his unique and paradoxical striving—
his grandeur and wretchedness, his capacity for questioning and crime,
his passion for death, his rocketing thrust toward the stars,
his doom and rebel glory.
All that, however, is merely a favorite theme for theologians,
or fuddled nay-sayers, or Hobbsian cynics.

Yes.     And it does seem a little mean-spirited,
a little lacking in the elementary courtesy
you expect from a departing guest,
to leave what were after all fantastically beautiful revels—
and to leave them blaming the management
(simply because you don't believe in Golden Ages)
for your own gluttony and savage rudeness.
The other guests, to be sure, are quite a different matter.
If we are all robots, if Life itself is a machine,
there is indeed some "radical flaw" in the arrangements,
some basic error in the calculations
of top-level engineering.

But in spite of Saint Paul, Augustine, and the Calvinists . . .

(All of whom, incidentally, blame women, and especially "Mother Eve,"
for throwing perfection out of gear)

nearly all women, most artists—female or male—
and other men who have managed to develop
their gifts of imagination and compassion—
all these know Life to be a mystery: pure miracle, not machine.
It even looks like a gift, a gift of freedom,
with freedom's only duty, given its time and place,
to find its own meaning.

Then shall we blame our twentieth-century culture—
heir of all the incredible nightmares of history
(including the recent explosions of indigestible people,
unmanageable information, and the Bomb)—
for giving into weak hands the Saturday night special
and other more frightening engines of death?

This is the jargon of social science, which always stumbles
over the obvious. For now we find all around us
merely some hideous heightening of an old malfunction
of minds and institutions.    This tempts your social engineer,
who still believes, it seems, in a Golden Age coming.
All it takes now, he thinks, is a bit of political tinkering,
a little genetic manipulation by experts,
and some degree of cultural restructuring—
managed, one fears, by professors of education
or leaders of the Moral Majority.
What sterile words!    What a dreary blueprint!

And what a dull masculine science!
that can never see how its schemes would merely worsen
that ancient disorder of mastery and submission
that has sent all the great cultures onto the ash-heap
for nearly ten thousand years;
that can look so far down Time's receding tracks
yet never guess how near the broken bridge—
how near humanity's leap toward some quite probable horror
that is probably quite beyond imagination.

There is then no hope at all?

Ah . . . hope. Well, hope.    Yes, there is always hope. . . .
"While there is life . . . "    you know how the saying goes.

# World Sacrifice

**1**

O loveliest, afloat around the sun
in her blue bubble—her jeweled atmosphere—
she catches the breath with her strange splendor
seen now at last from space.

Her mystery stupefies and stops the mind
looking for origins; surely she has been woven
out of the all-embracing mystery of the real.
Call this a random universe if you must,
for clearly a shuffled deck of cards will never
reorder itself, and time's arrow of direction
flies toward a distant dark and absolute zero;
but on the way what miracle, what wonder!
from that first flash—eternally improbable—
that burst of Light, or Fire, through intricate ballets,
wave-particle events that danced to form
trillions on trillions of galaxies, then stars—
among them ours—and here, among these planets,
lonely, sapphire, and fragile—again ours.

Floating, O loveliest, in her blue bubble . . .
whose deepest mystery, however
lies not in her sweet numinous presence here,
nor in that first live cell, shocked into being
somehow, by ray or lightning, but in the web
of living forms that followed—endless variety
woven of oneness: think how the genes of algae
(given some difference in complexity)
work like the snake's, the porpoise's, and ours.

And yet, we are told, our own genetic messages
are broken by something queer—they call it "meaningless"—
long strips of empty intervening sequences
science cannot decode.    It just might be, however,
that there's a blank check Nature has handed over
to our unfinished species
where we might write our future and the Earth's.

**2**
She has given us clues, hints of a living whole
wherein no solitary form survives:
where the cells of human bodies
depend on micro-aliens; where green plants
let out their cells to photosynthetic lodgers
so that the sun may feed them     and feed us
not only food but air; where predator and prey,
rain and rain forest, move in a strict balance.

Then with sacrifice as companion all these peoples
come out of mystery into the great world rite:
aware or not (old species, like the whales,
seem more aware than we), willing or not,
all die for other life, live on the death of others.
Exquisite web and fragile, man has torn you
almost beyond repair.     Long has he taken
("winner take all") with no exchange, no giving
back to the living wholeness.     Look, now, the desert is creeping
stealthy and sure across the desiccated
fields of his progress.     Look how, like Nero—
idiot Nero, who tore his mother's womb
to see where he was got—he is still ravaging
her depths, soiling her surface, who first received him
into her arms.     Late-born among her children.

**3**
Now they are going
those others
and bewildered
eyes that see dimly
in pain or hunger
search vainly
old havens once felt as home
not enemy territory.

They come out of mystery
into the arms of Earth-life
and find
not the old fertile embrace of life-and-death
but only
Death.

What can we say to you
who are going before us?
We cannot even sit beside you
infant whale
cast up on the gritty sands
our poisons in your blood.

We ought to be able to touch you
with the tenderness
of a grieving mother
if we loved enough
we might share your fading
memories of song
your memories
of your own cherishing mother

we could sing other songs to you
our own songs of a day
when Life was a mother.
What can we say now
to all who are leaving
before us?

How can we comfort you
harp seal mother
sobbing, ripped open with grief,
where snow is red
your once beautiful baby
bloody
flayed utterly
still living?
Can we hope to persuade you
that this was necessary
this sacrifice
a part of the great world rite
this offering to a furrier's greed
and to that deeper lust of our modern Moloch
the death-desiring hunger
of macho human creatures
with their singular "rites of passage"?

What can we ever say to you
who are going before us?

Out of approaching silence
a diminished thunder
of arriving wings

One robin is chirping today
merrily
on my city lawn
where once there were ten,
And in wilder haunts
singers who come to feed
linger to die
silvery intervals
of reed or horn
hover and are still
Even if we loved enough
we could not comfort such wildness
and the eagle
the fierce falcon
would spurn us rightly.

Emblems
of another music . . .
of our vanishing freedom . . .
in your going
it is ourselves we mourn.
Must we say to you,
"We can live without birds?"

**4**
A long procession
hopeless
they leave us now
those great perfected species.
True, they have always been going
but they have gone slowly
fading into the flux of the future
always to be replaced
by those who restored the balance.

If they killed it was only for need
and the lion walked harmless near the herd
when he had no hunger.

Now in their silent departure
they look back
they wait a little
the great sequoias withering
the rain forests dying
and a long sigh seems to tremble
on the polluted air
a question they who present it
may never understand
nor this victorious species . . .
ours.

Oh, when will you be finished?
What have you given?
What did you ever have to give?

Species more lethal than the tiger
but far less beautiful
can the murderous spawn of your cities
replace that      fearful symmetry
with another less terrible
but just as perfect?

Your tanks are more powerful
than the great gray elephant
but they have never moved
with his lumbering grace
they are not directed by his wisdom.

You have fingers
which the dolphins have not
and fingers create writing
and technology
but can your vaunted structures
of social organization
equal the playful intelligent harmony
of this finer species
the compassion      the Confucian good manners

the hatred of falsehood
the subtle effectiveness in education
the delicate interpersonal complexities
the love without guilt and fear?

We were not here only
for an organic balance
for the fertility of Earth
we were here also for a deeper reason
you have not fathomed.

Oh, when will you be finished?

**5**
Shall we then say to you
who are going before us:

We too have shared in the
great world rite.

True, we have killed
but only for need.
We needed the earth
and we took it.
We were told, so we thought, to be fruitful
and we were
(look at those towers, those arsenals of steel and information)
and to multiply
Oh, how we did
(those millions of gaunt
bloat-bellied hollow-eyed
children)
We needed the earth
and we took it.
Now we no longer need you.
Before long science will feed us.

But we know all that to be falsehood.
We were also "told" (and somehow we knew it)
to replenish the Earth
and there were other possible choices
not made

for reasons we need not go into
here.
There were roads not taken
not this unending
ever-widening asphalt
but roads wandering away from
all this desert
into a green freedom
half wilderness

Go then and tell them
who have vanished before you
into the dim fastnesses
of a darker garden
tell them
the irreplaceable
who wait for you
that in truth we no longer need you
as sacrifice.
Soon science will feed us
more than we hoped for.

Tell them who wait for you
and for us
yes, and for Her
floating, O loveliest, around the sun
tell them
we are almost finished.

## Strict Is the Charge

Strict is the charge upon the ear, the eye.
Help will not cancel such a charge
                              no priestly power
to absolve will cancel
                      nor that hard-won,     sour
dispiriting     ego-knowledge men call therapy.
Then boldly charge the mind
                      that faltering will
still boldly charge
                coldly break
                            until
haunted perspectives open,
                    echo, and enlarge.
Strict is the charge upon the
                          haunted ear and eye.

                                    Palm Sunday, 1983